OUR WISH LIST

Make a WISH... *then make it come true,* TOGETHER.

We sometimes forget that this is something we can do—that no matter what life holds today, there is always a lot that the two of you can change... a lot that you can make happen... a lot that you can bring into being.

When it comes to the wishes on these pages, start where you feel drawn to start, talk this through together; let your shared enthusiasm guide you. Whether this book takes you a year to complete or the rest of your lives, let it remind you what's possible. And whether or not you're able to make each of these wishes come true, just their existence can show you that even the most ordinary day is full of potential. Because the very process of making a wish has a way of changing what's around you.

Our Wish List

EVERYDAY WISHES

a wish we'll get to live with every day

a wish we can make come true right away

a wish that costs nothing

a wish that's a compromise

a wish to be a tourist close to home

WISHES FOR AND ABOUT US

a wish our past selves would appreciate

a wish that's just between us

a wish to create a new ritual or tradition together

a wish our future selves will appreciate

a wish that celebrates us, and what we've done so far

WISHES FOR CONNECTION

a wish come true for someone else

a wish that's a request

a wish other people are in on

a wish to make an impact

WISHES FOR EXPERIENCES

a wish to re-create a favorite moment

a wish we'll need to get dressed up for

a wish to learn something together

a wish for a start-to-finish perfect day

BIG WISHES

a wish that will take some effort

a wish that will keep growing

a wish that takes us both out of our comfort zone

a wish to honor a milestone

SPECIAL KINDS OF WISHES

a wish to brighten a cloudy day

a wish we'll get a souvenir from

a wish that feels impractical

a wish for a special day apart

a wish to keep going

EVERYDAY WISHES

A wish is a way of looking at the world. It takes an ordinary day and sees what could be. A wish doesn't have to be huge to be impactful... and it doesn't have to take a lot of effort to change things powerfully. Make a wish together—one that's close to home, one that changes today in the best way, one that sees the possibility in what is here already.

A dream
you dream
TOGETHER
is reality.

YOKO ONO

A wish we'll get to live with every day

An herb garden, a built-in bookshelf, a porch swing for your morning coffee—there's an idea you've had that will change your home and life so beautifully. Give it an evening or a weekend or two to bring it into being; this is the perfect time to add a little something.

The date we made this wish come true:

THE WISH:

WHAT WE LOOK FORWARD TO ONCE THIS WISH COMES TRUE:

WHAT WE WANT TO CAPTURE AND REMEMBER:

We have more
POSSIBILITIES
available in each
MOMENT *than*
we realize.

THICH NHAT HANH

A wish we can make come true right away

This very minute, there's a wish that's within reach—a change of evening plans, a movie you've been wanting to watch, a dinner date, a small purchase you've been waiting to make. Here is your invitation to seize the moment... to remember that right now might be a very good time to make a wish come true.

The date we made this wish come true:

THE WISH:

WHAT IT HELPED US TO REALIZE:

WHAT WE WANT TO CAPTURE AND REMEMBER:

The BEST *things in* LIFE *are free.*

LEW BROWN & BUDDY DE SYLVA

A wish that costs nothing

Not all wishes have to be bought—some of the most memorable wishes cost absolutely nothing. Pack a picnic with what's in the fridge, and take it to the beach. Listen to a favorite album while reminiscing. Lie in the backyard and watch the sky change. What free experience is waiting to become a favorite memory?

The date we made this wish come true:

THE WISH:

THE THING WE LOVED MOST ABOUT IT:

WHAT WE WANT TO CAPTURE AND REMEMBER:

...hold onto that MIDDLE *ground... it's in there that* THE MAGIC *happens.*

SUSAN BRANCH

A wish that's a compromise

Maybe one of you wants a beach vacation, while the other wants a city escape. Maybe one of you wants a night out at a concert, while the other wants to head to a baseball game. The next time it seems your wishes don't match up, make it a point to find a creative middle ground—a compromise that isn't just "good enough," it's actually wonderful for everyone.

The date we made this wish come true:

THE WISH:

WHAT EACH OF US INITIALLY WANTED INSTEAD:

WHAT WE WANT TO CAPTURE AND REMEMBER:

...LOOK FOR *the extraordinary in* ORDINARY *things...*

BALTHUS

A wish to be a tourist close to home

There's something nearby that comes highly recommended... And yet, you've never been. It might be a tourist attraction, a scenic spot, a special-occasion restaurant. "Someday," you've always told yourselves. What if someday is now?

The date we made this wish come true:

THE WISH:

WHAT WE THOUGHT WE'D LIKE ABOUT IT:

WHAT WE WANT TO CAPTURE AND REMEMBER:

WISHES FOR AND ABOUT US

A wish can build a world within the larger world, with just enough room for two. It can create something wonderful that isn’t for everyone to see—and that is part of its strength. Wishes like this are the ones that remind you who you are together. They connect one heart to another heart. And they touch into something that’s always been here: your joy, your potential, your spark.

...DREAMS

don't have an expiration date.

DAVID NIVEN

A wish our past selves would appreciate

There's a wish you would have wanted to make come true long ago, but circumstances just weren't right. Maybe you didn't have the time, the skills, the tools, or the money... But now you do. Get in touch with your younger selves, and help make their old wish come true.

The date we made this wish come true:

THE WISH:

WHY WE COULDN'T MAKE IT HAPPEN EARLIER:

WHAT WE WANT TO CAPTURE AND REMEMBER:

The HUMAN HEART *has hidden treasures...*

CHARLOTTE BRONTË

A wish that's just between us

There's something special about a shared secret, no matter how big or small—a spark of excitement in an experience that no one else will hear about. What's something you've been wanting to do that will only ever be shared between the two of you?

The date we made this wish come true:

THE WISH:

WHAT WE LOVE ABOUT KEEPING THIS BETWEEN US:

WHAT WE WANT TO CAPTURE AND REMEMBER:

YOUR
life is an
OCCASION.

SUZANNE WEYN

A wish to create a new ritual or tradition together

There's something delightful in predictability—a quiet joy in knowing what to expect, a comfort in "the way things have always been." What new tradition do you want to create? Whether weekly, monthly, seasonally, or annually, give yourself something to look forward to—something new that will one day feel like it's always been this way.

The date we made this wish come true:

THE WISH:

WE HOPE THIS RITUAL HELPS US FEEL:

WHAT WE WANT TO CAPTURE AND REMEMBER:

The beginning is ALWAYS TODAY.

MARY SHELLEY

A wish our future selves will appreciate

Some wishes are more like seeds—they're actions we take today for the harvest we will gather in a few seasons. And even if they don't feel like this moment's highest priority, your future selves will look back with gratitude. Think ahead just a bit... What can you begin today that will become a future wish come true?

The date we made this wish come true:

THE WISH:

WHAT THIS WISH WILL MAKE POSSIBLE FOR US IN THE FUTURE:

WHAT WE WANT TO CAPTURE AND REMEMBER:

Take time to CELEBRATE...

JOHN O'DONOHUE

A wish that celebrates us, and what we've done so far

In the time you've been together, there is so much you've done, so much you've figured out, so many ways you've grown. Offer yourselves a moment to celebrate all of it. Whether it's an evening of writing down your accomplishments or a celebratory dinner, take time to appreciate everything.

The date we made this wish come true:

THE WISH:

A FEW OF THE THINGS WE WANT TO CELEBRATE:

WHAT WE WANT TO CAPTURE AND REMEMBER:

WISHES FOR CONNECTION

These are the wishes that want to be part of a bigger story—the wishes that shine brighter when they're shared. They may start small, but they ripple outward until they have a broader impact... until they reach a larger community. By the time these wishes have come true, they've traveled further than you might have imagined. This is both their power and their beauty.

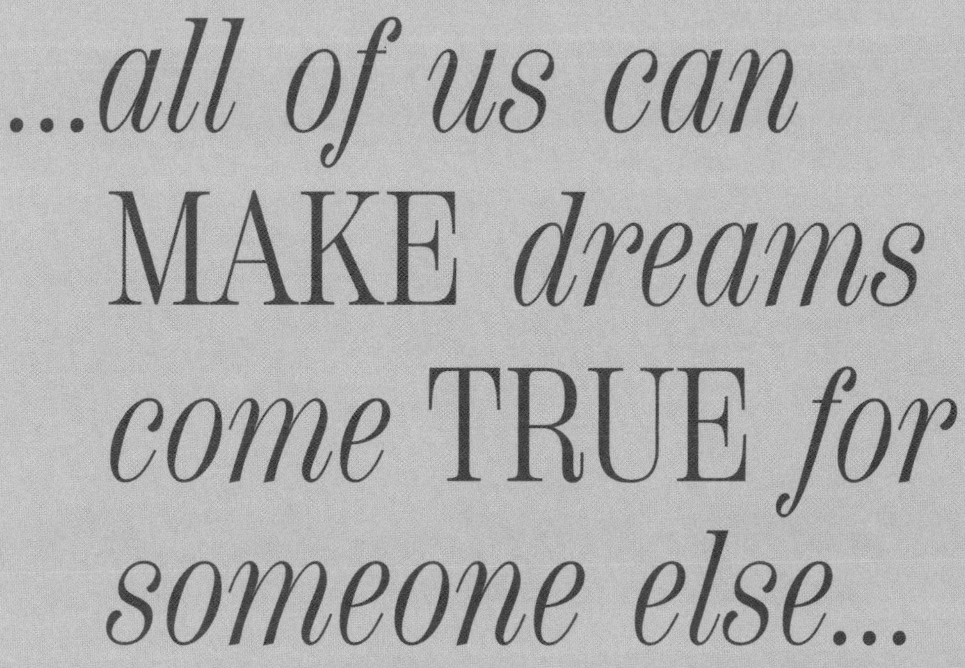

SHARON SHINN

A wish come true for someone else

There's a wish, spoken or unspoken, that isn't yours. But it's one you know about. Maybe it belongs to someone in your family, or your circle of friends, your neighborhood, your larger community. It's a wish you have the resources and the ability to make true. And right here is where you do.

The date we made this wish come true:

THE WISH:

HOW WE FEEL ABOUT FACILITATING THIS:

WHAT WE WANT TO CAPTURE AND REMEMBER:

Sometimes, all you have to do IS ASK...

RANDY PAUSCH

A wish that's a request

There's at least one important wish you can't fulfill without the help of someone else—maybe you need their skills, or their resources, their time, their extra pair of hands, their expertise. Give them a chance to help out in just the way you need.

The date we made this wish come true:

THE WISH:

SOME THOUGHTS AND FEELINGS WE HAVE ABOUT ASKING:

WHAT WE WANT TO CAPTURE AND REMEMBER:

This is the power of gathering: it INSPIRES *us... to be more hopeful, more joyful... more* ALIVE.

ALICE WATERS

A wish other people are in on

This is a wish with an invitation attached—a wish to gather some important people together. It could be a small group or a large party, a virtual gathering or an in-person one, a "just because" or an occasion worth celebrating. In this moment, what feels like the most perfect gathering?

The date we made this wish come true:

THE WISH:

WHO WE ARE INVITING:

WHAT WE WANT TO CAPTURE AND REMEMBER:

Do your
LITTLE *bit*
of GOOD *where*
you are...

DESMOND TUTU

A wish to make an impact

Some resource you have a little extra of is just waiting to plug in to the world's needs. Whether it's a few hours a week to spend volunteering, a portion of a paycheck to donate to a cause you appreciate, or a skill you can use in service somewhere, there's a difference you're about to make—no matter how small or how big.

The date we made this wish come true:

THE WISH:

WHAT WE HOPE THIS WISH MAKES POSSIBLE FOR SOMEONE ELSE:

WHAT WE WANT TO CAPTURE AND REMEMBER:

WISHES FOR EXPERIENCES

Not every wish is here to offer tangible things... Some are here to offer moments worth remembering—the kinds of times that make us think *hang on to this*, even as we live them. These are the wishes that create bright afternoons, evenings we don't want to end, hours to cherish, and memories we know we'll return to again and again.

How LUCKY WE ARE *to have such a treasure of memories.*

LADY BIRD JOHNSON

A wish to re-create a favorite moment

A first date, a favorite date, a moment that has become a beloved memory… there are so many important days and nights in your shared history. What's one you'd like to live again—one that makes you both light up when you think about the chance to repeat it?

The date we made this wish come true:

THE WISH:

A LITTLE BIT ABOUT THE FIRST TIME WE LIVED IT:

WHAT WE WANT TO CAPTURE AND REMEMBER:

BEING *alive* is *the* SPECIAL *occasion.*

MARY ENGELBREIT

A wish we'll need to get dressed up for

Whether it's an evening out or an evening in, let it be special. Get a little fancy. Make it into an occasion. Get butterflies when you look at each other, and remember all over again how your story began.

The date we made this wish come true:

THE WISH:

WHAT EACH OF US DID TO GET READY:

WHAT WE WANT TO CAPTURE AND REMEMBER:

...together
WE CAN
do so much.

HELEN KELLER

A wish to learn something together

Be beginners at something together: a cooking class, a dancing lesson, a new language, a skill you can cultivate from scratch. It's not about being good right away, it's about growing side by side, deciding to try, and the joy of discovering something that's new to both of you.

The date we made this wish come true:

THE WISH:

HOW OR WHY WE CHOSE IT:

WHAT WE WANT TO CAPTURE AND REMEMBER:

I hope there are days when you fall in LOVE *with being* ALIVE.

BROOKE HAMPTON

A wish for a start-to-finish perfect day

A day that holds all the good things... What does it look like? What's for breakfast? Where do you go after that, and what happens next? Whether simple and close to home or a little more complex, map out a day from beginning to end and then make it happen.

The date we made this wish come true:

THE WISH:

THE PART OF THE DAY WE MOST LOOK FORWARD TO:

WHAT WE WANT TO CAPTURE AND REMEMBER:

BIG WISHES

Some wishes require a little something extra on their way to coming true. They ask us to work for them a bit... But that process doesn't have to feel like a chore—it can be a reminder that the things we want most deeply are worth showing up for. These are the wishes that change us every step of the way—by reminding us that effort can alter the course of our days.

Be willing
to go all out
in PURSUIT *of*
your DREAM.

LES BROWN

A wish that will take some effort

Wishes for the long-term take some time, patience, and planning; this can mean it's hard to get started on them because they often seem a bit daunting. What's a big wish you've been drawn to... and a small (or even tiny!) thing you can do today to begin to make it come true?

The date we made the bigger wish come true:

THE WISH:

ONE STEP WE JUST TOOK TOWARD IT:

WHAT WE WANT TO CAPTURE AND REMEMBER:

Every REAL *story is a* NEVER-ENDING *story.*

MICHAEL ENDE

A wish that will keep growing

Once in a while, you can make a wish that's endless—a wish that just wants to keep growing. Whether it's a wish to learn a new language together, a wish to communicate better and better, a wish to show up for each other more fully, these wishes may never come to a stopping point... But that's the best part. What's a process you never want to end? Right here is where you can start.

The date we began to make this wish come true:

THE WISH:

HOW WE IMAGINE IT WILL CHANGE US:

WHAT WE WANT TO CAPTURE AND REMEMBER:

The dream is to keep SURPRISING *yourself...*

TOM HIDDLESTON

A wish that takes us both out of our comfort zone

There's a wish that makes you both a little uncomfortable… in a good way. It's a wish with some growth, some surprise, or some challenge built in. Give yourselves the chance to do something you've never done before. Follow the trail of a wish that's been calling your name. See what happens when you move beyond the everyday.

The date we made this wish come true:

THE WISH:

ALL THE THINGS WE FEEL ABOUT IT:

WHAT WE WANT TO CAPTURE AND REMEMBER:

The GREAT *goal should be to* CELEBRATE *along the way...*

DOROTHY LIVESAY

A wish to honor a milestone

However long you've been together, you have your own collection of milestones, personal holidays, and anniversaries. Choose one you want to honor and celebrate in a special way the next time it comes around... What's the perfect way to commemorate the significance of this important day?

The date we made this wish come true:

THE WISH:

WHAT THIS MILESTONE MEANS TO US:

WHAT WE WANT TO CAPTURE AND REMEMBER:

SPECIAL KINDS OF WISHES

Some wishes remind you just how much is possible. They inspire you to relate to the world differently—with lightheartedness, creativity, joy, sincerity. These are the wishes that spark more wishes, by reminding you that when you think outside the ordinary, the world responds to your energy and your effort in surprising ways.

Who cares about the clouds when we're TOGETHER?

DALE EVANS

A wish to brighten a cloudy day

Maybe it's a true rainy day, or maybe it's a day when everything has gone wrong and things are in need of some serious brightening. What's a wish you want to make and set aside for a time when you most need it?

The date we made this wish come true:

THE WISH:

THE SITUATION THAT REQUIRED US TO USE IT:

WHAT WE WANT TO CAPTURE AND REMEMBER:

Let EACH DAY *be a day to remember...*

MELODY BEATTIE

A wish we'll get a souvenir from

A pebble, a trinket, a photograph to frame—some days have an opportunity for a memory built in. Some places offer you a little piece of themselves to take home. Start with the souvenir in mind: What's a treasure you want to bring home, and the wish that will help you get it there?

The date we made this wish come true:

THE WISH:

THE MEMENTO WE'LL GET TO KEEP:

WHAT WE WANT TO CAPTURE AND REMEMBER:

BE DARING,
be different,
be impractical...

CECIL BEATON

A wish that feels impractical

Silly, frivolous, unnecessary... this is the place for any or all of those things. This is the time for a wish you said no to at least once already. Let it show you the magic you almost didn't get a chance to experience.

The date we made this wish come true:

THE WISH:

WHY WE ALMOST IGNORED IT:

WHAT WE WANT TO CAPTURE AND REMEMBER:

Let there be
SPACES *in your*
togetherness...

KAHLIL GIBRAN

A wish for a special day apart

Closeness isn't just created in moments together—it's created in moments apart. This is an invitation for each of you to design the perfect day on your own—a day that's just for you... a day that welcomes yourself, your needs, your preferences. Make time to connect when the day is done to cherish sharing everything that each of you got to do.

The date we made these wishes come true:

______________________'S WISH:

______________________'S WISH:

WHAT WE WANT TO CAPTURE AND REMEMBER:

My wish for you is that you continue. Continue to be WHO *and how* YOU ARE...

MAYA ANGELOU

A wish to keep going

So much of what you're doing is already good. So much of the way you *are* is already the way you would *want to be*. Sometimes a wish isn't about doing something differently, it's about making sure to do more of what you're doing already. What's a way of being that you want to make sure you continue?

The date we made our intention to continue:

THE WISH:

HOW LONG WE'VE BEEN DOING THIS TOGETHER:

WHAT WE WANT TO CAPTURE AND REMEMBER:

The world is a possibility if only YOU'LL DISCOVER *it.*

RALPH ELLISON

A shared library of even more wishes

THE WISH:

The date we made this wish come true:

What we want to capture and remember:

THE WISH:

The date we made this wish come true:

What we want to capture and remember:

THE WISH:

The date we made this wish come true:

What we want to capture and remember:

THE WISH:

The date we made this wish come true:

What we want to capture and remember:

REMEMBER *those wonderful* MOMENTS *you have had.*

SRI SRI RAVI SHANKAR

Thoughts, notes, and things to hold on to

Thoughts, notes, and things to hold on to

An imprint of the Crown Publishing Group
A division of Penguin Random House LLC
1745 Broadway, New York, NY 10019
live-inspired.com | penguinrandomhouse.com

ISBN: 978-1-957891-65-1

Writer: M.H. Clark
Designer: Steve Potter
Editor: Miriam Hathaway
Production Manager: Olivia Holmes

1st printing. Manufactured in China with soy inks on FSC®-Mix certified paper.

The authorized representative in the EU for product safety and compliance is Penguin Random House Ireland, Morrison Chambers, 32 Nassau Street, Dublin D02 YH68, Ireland, https://eu-contact.penguin.ie.

Create meaningful moments with gifts that inspire.

CONNECT WITH US
live-inspired.com | sayhello@compendiuminc.com

@compendiumliveinspired
#compendiumliveinspired